THEN & NOW®

WASHINGTON COUNTY

OPPOSITE: Virginia Route 91 enters Washington County at Johnson County, Tennessee, a little more than a mile south of Damascus, on March 17, 1949. This road has since been widened and made into a divided highway, and the welcome sign has been replaced with a more modern, glossy sign. (Courtesy of Robert N. Monroe, Virginia Department of Transportation.)

THEN & NOW®

WASHINGTON COUNTY

Joe Tennis with the

Historical Society of Washington County, VA

ISBN 978-0-7385-9211-4

Library of Congress Control Number: 2011934515

Published by Arcadia Publishing
Charleston, South Carolina

Printed in the United States of America

For all general information, please contact Arcadia Publishing:
Telephone 843-853-2070
Fax 843-853-0044
E-mail sales@arcadiapublishing.com

Visit us on the Internet at www.arcadiapublishing.com

On the Cover: Around 1905, the president of the Virginia-Carolina Railway, Wilton Egerton Mingea, arranged an outing of Abingdon-area businessmen and officials to showcase locations along his railroad—nicknamed "The Virginia Creeper" either for the presence of Virginia creeper vines or because of how slowly its trains climbed steep grades. These men pose near a wooden trestle crossing Whitetop Laurel Creek on what is now Bridge 21 of the Virginia Creeper Trail. Trains stopped running on this railroad line, later called the Abingdon Branch of the Norfolk & Western Railway, in 1977. The trail opened on the rail bed in 1987. Bridge 21 was installed in 2002 after a flood destroyed the old trestle on July 29, 2001. (Then image courtesy of Jerry Goodpasture and the Historical Society of Washington County, Virginia; Now photograph by Joe Tennis.)

On the Back Cover: Washington Springs Hotel, shown in 1929, opened prior to the Civil War at a site near Walker Mountain, a couple of miles northeast of Glade Spring. The resort served several types of springwater but closed by the time the hotel burned down in the 1970s. The hotel site has since returned to wilderness. (Courtesy of the Virginia Tech Library.)

Contents

For Melissa and James Caudill, John Wolfe, and Amy Fleenor—your stories of South Holston Lake, Abingdon, Emory, Green Spring, Washington County, and Virginia have been a great inspiration

Acknowledgments

Foremost thanks go to Melissa Watson and Jane Oakes at the Historical Society of Washington County, Virginia; Bill McKee, who offered invaluable assistance, photographs, and scanning expertise; and Shelby Edwards, who allowed me to borrow postcards and who had initially encouraged me to pursue a project on Washington County. I also most sincerely thank Bob McCracken, who generously shared slides as well as a shuttle; and Eleanor Grasselli, an optimistic cheerleader for this often challenging venture.

Many others provided information and images, including Jerry Goodpasture, Joseph Russ, Charles Seaver, Michelle Earl, Robert N. Monroe, David Patton, Marc Brodsky, Jennifer McDaid, George Stone, Sue Thomas, Nancy Leasure, Susie Montgomery, Ray Mullins, May Joe Craig, Bruce Waters, Gail Fleenor, Donald F. White, Robert and Anne Duncan, Kathy Shearer, Karen Fitzpatrick Hall, Kitty Henninger, Martha Keys, Will Stein, Paul Moore, Joe Smith, Janice Snead, Colleen Davenport Taylor, Cynthia Long, Jerry Belisle, Joan Sutherland, Margaret Duff Alexander, Connie C. Miller, Anna Elliott, Harry Haynes, June Faris, Don Smith, Donna Price, Sidney Hal Parker, Richard Kretz, V.N. "Bud" Phillips, Frank Kilgore, Jean Kilgore, Bob Preston, Daniel Gray Preston, Nancy Lamb, Charlie Barnette, Regina Green, Carmen Blevins, Rubinette Niemann, Douglas Ogle, Richard Rose, Leah Prater, Jerry Ivey, Tim Buchanan, Matt Crum, Teresa Harless, Ray Mullins, Gerald and Nancy Booher, Dirk Moore, Robert Vejnar, Anne Dunham, Joella Barbour, Jan Rainero, Wayne Sheffey, Richard Smith, Kim Roberts, Beth Merz, Kenny Fannon, Ken Marsh, Tom Horsch, Gary Greer, Helen Galliher, James and Annette Goode, Beverly Fitzpatrick Jr., and Skip Blackburn.

I also thank friends and colleagues who provided advice and patience, especially Carol Jackson, David McGee, Jan Patrick, Tim Cable, Donnamarie Emmert, Cara Ellen Modisett, Kurt Rheinheimer, Hannah Cassilly, Linda Hoagland, Anne West, Kathryn Nichols, Darlene Cole, Donna Fee, Rex and Lisa McCarty, Kyle and Jenny Buckland, Robert DeBord, Tony and Tammy Balthis, Ken Heath, Brenda Sullins, Chris Counts, Peggy Hensley, Patsy Phillips, Daniel Rodgers, Tom Perry, Susan J. Harrington, Doris and Larry Musick, Emily McCarty, and Jeannette F. Foist.

Further kudos go to the staff at Arcadia, including Maggie Bullwinkel, Elizabeth Bray, Lindsay Carter, Tim Sumerel, and Brinkley Taliaferro.

Additional thanks go to family members, especially Maggie Caudill; Steve and Stephanie Talbert; Rob and Michelle Tennis; Jo Boswell; my parents, Richard and Jeanette Tennis; my wife, Mary; my daughter, Abigail; and my son, John Patrick, who endured a rainy road trip and a two-mile hike to "The Train" but still came home with a smile.

Then images are credited throughout the text to their respective contributors; photographs provided by the Historical Society of Washington County, Virginia, are simply credited to HSWCV. Unless otherwise stated, all Now photographs are by Joe Tennis.

Bibliography

Adkins, Leonard M. *50 Hikes in Southern Virginia: From the Cumberland Gap to the Atlantic Ocean.* Woodstock, VT: Countryman Press, 2002.

Blackburn, M.L. "Washington County Dam-Lake Project Taking Shape." *Bristol Herald Courier*, May 16, 1980.

Blevins, Thomas H. *A Brief History of the "Virginia Creeper."* Self-published, 2003.

Davis, Edward H., and Edward B. Morgan. *The Virginia Creeper Trail Companion: Nature and History Along Southwest Virginia's National Recreation Trail.* Johnson City, TN: Overmountain Press, 1997.

Herman, Bernard L. "Washington County Grist Mills." *The Historical Society of Washington County, Va. Publication Series II, No. 12, 1974–75.* Abingdon, VA: Historical Society of Washington County, Virginia Inc., 1975.

Kearfott, Clarence Baker. *Highland Mills.* New York: Vantage Press, 1970.

King, Nanci C. *Places In Time, Volume I.* Abingdon, VA: Abingdon Printing Services, 1989.

———. *Places In Time, Volume II.* Marion, VA: Tucker Printing, 1994.

———. *Places In Time, Volume III.* Marion, VA: Tucker Printing, 1997.

Hall, Louise Fortune. *A History of Damascus: 1793–1950.* Abingdon, VA: John Anderson Press, 1950.

Hall, Louise Fortune and Marilou Hall Preston. *History of Damascus, Virginia: 1950–1978.* Bristol, VA: Quality Printers, 1978.

Loth, Calder, ed. *The Virginia Landmarks Register, Fourth Edition.* Charlottesville, VA: University of Virginia Press, 1999.

Neal, J. Allen. *Bicentennial History of Washington County, Virginia, 1776–1976.* Dallas: Taylor Publishing, 1977.

Sexton, Daveena. "Group Planning Altamont's Restoration." *Washington County News*, September 5, 1990.

Introduction

It was 1776, the same year the Declaration of Independence was drafted and signed. The capitol of Virginia stood at Williamsburg, and Patrick Henry was elected the first nonroyal governor of the Old Dominion. That same year, tiny Black's Fort in southwest Virginia was named the courthouse town for a vast span of wilderness stretching as far west as the Cumberland Mountains along what is now the Kentucky border. In that wilderness, battles continually raged between early settlers and Native Americans over land use and ownership. As 1777 dawned, the first court was held at Washington County, a place named for Gen. George Washington, the future first president of the United States.

In 1778, Black's Fort became Abingdon—a village with a name likely derived from Martha Washington's ancestral parish in England. Situated at the crossroads of several trading routes, Abingdon grew increasingly important in the days of the Great Stage Road, which traversed the modern-day routes of US Highway 11 and Interstate 81. Then, in 1856, came the railroad, which eventually opened three major spur lines across Washington County to reach Litz, Hanckel, and Saltville; Haskell Station, Wolf Run, and Abrams Falls; and Delmar, Drowning Ford, Damascus, and Creek Junction.

Located east of the legendary Virginia coalfields, Washington County invites visitors to a valley nestled between towering Brumley Mountain and the mile-high peaks of Whitetop Mountain and Mount Rogers. The courthouse town of Abingdon contains the Barter Theatre, designated as the State Theatre of Virginia, and the mammoth Martha Washington Inn, a private home that once served as a women's college and a temporary Civil War hospital. Along its seemingly endless acres of fields and forests, Washington County boasts pieces of paradise ranging from a hidden lake at the Hidden Valley Wildlife Management Area to the world-famous Appalachian Trail, nearly all of the 34-mile Virginia Creeper Trail, the refreshing waters of South Holston Lake, the back roads and byways crossing Clinch Mountain, and the toe-tapping tunes along The Crooked Road: Virginia's Heritage Music Trail.

Today, at 566 square miles, Washington County is the largest Virginia county southwest of Roanoke. Villages scattered across this scenic heart of the highlands include Mendota, a once-incorporated town named for "a bend in the river," and Meadowview, another once-incorporated community, located along the main line of railroad tracks linking Roanoke to Bristol. Emory & Henry College stands about 10 miles from the county courthouse, while the scenic town of Damascus, just north of the Tennessee border, provides a gateway to the Mount Rogers National Recreation Area.

Three forks of the Holston River course through Washington County, with waters that eventually drain to the Mississippi River. Along these branches and their arms of creeks and streams once stood the many mills of the Mountain Empire. Some creeks, it is said, could hardly get out of one millpond before jumping into another, and maps still note milling operations at DeBusk Mill, Parks Mill, Craigs Mill, King's Mill, Vails Mill, and White's Mill.

Trees inspired the names of Chestnut Ridge, Chestnut Mountain, and Chestnut Grove Church. More tree names crop up at Beech Mountain, Beech Creek, Cedar Bluff, and Cedarville. Wild plums likely inspired the name Plum Creek, while the laurels covering creek banks are remembered at Laurel Creek, a rocky watercourse dashing through Damascus and called the Laurel River through the early 1900s.

Wild animals lent names to Washington County at Wolf Run in the west, Beaverdam Creek in the east, and Goose Creek in between. Raccoon Valley lies between River Ridge and Smith Creek. Turkey Knob rises on Clinch Mountain, near Brumley Creek. Buzzard Rock, along the Appalachian Trail, is a formation of volcanic rock likely named for circling vultures commonly called buzzards. A tree once used as a bear's scratching post in eastern Washington County became known as the Bear Tree at the Bear Tree Gap of Straight Mountain, later giving its name to Beartree Lake and the Beartree Recreation Area.

Perhaps the most comical, or most legendary, tale explains how one crossroads came to be called Goose Pimple Junction. According to the story, an estranged couple living near Bristol would cuss and carry on, and, as longtime resident Russ Taylor once put it, it sounded like they were "raising the devil over there." All that noise, in turn, would incite goose pimples on whoever heard them.

By contrast, on the eastern side of the county, the friendly faces of farmers would naturally inspire the name "Friendship" for a community near the South Fork of the Holston River.

Family names are remembered at Widener Valley, Denton Valley, and Rhea Valley, as well as Rocktown, Roetown, Burson Place, Livingston Creek, and the Ketchum Branch. The Garrett family gave its name to Garrett Creek and its frothy Garrett Creek Cascades. The pioneering Fleenor brothers, in turn, came to Washington County in the late 1700s, and the family name remains on maps at Fleenors and Fleenor Spring.

Osceola takes its name from a Seminole chief. Konnarock appears to be the linguistic evolution of a rock cliff called the Corner Rock. And Zenobia? Well, this woodsy village near Clinch Mountain shares its name, for some reason, with a Syrian queen who led a famous revolt against the Roman Empire.

Some names change. Konnarock was once called Azen. Buena Vista became Plasterco. What was once called Stump, for postmaster Susan E. Stump, has evolved into greater Green Spring, while Hazelspring is now simply part of the Tumbling Creek section of Poor Valley. At Rocktown, road signs are labeled Jasper Creek, but maps say this same stream should be called Gaspard Creek.

One tale says some young men went to Texas and returned to rename their community Alvarado, replacing the earlier name of Barron, along the South Fork of the Holston River. Similarly, a longstanding story says some travelers took off for the Gold Rush on the Pacific Coast and, upon returning to their farming community between the middle and south forks of the Holston River, renamed it Lodi.

The hopes of extracting iron inspired the name of the Iron Mountain, near Damascus. A lime quarry left its mark at Lime Hill. The longstanding practice of boiling brine to produce salt led to the name Saltville along the Smyth County line. A spring resort serving alum water became Alum Wells. Many local communities, in turn, contain stories tied to Washington County's three R's—roads, rails, and rivers.

Children playing in a spring found yellow gravel, providing inspiration for the colorful name "Yellow Springs." Various crossroads came to be called Blacksburg, Blackwell, Whiterock Branch, and Whitetop Mountain. Washington County also seems to have gotten an early start on "going green," with Green Cove, Greendale, Green Spring, and Greenway Creek—plus not one, but two places called Greenfield.

From Clinch Mountain to Konnarock, and from Three Springs to Glade Spring, Then & Now: *Washington County* highlights the history and beauty of this mountainous land, showing images from the late 1800s to the late 1900s contrasted with contemporary photographs of Washington County as it appears today. It is a journey of wild waters, wild wonders, side-of-the-road stories, and, yes, even a few legends.

CHAPTER 1

HEART OF THE HIGHLANDS

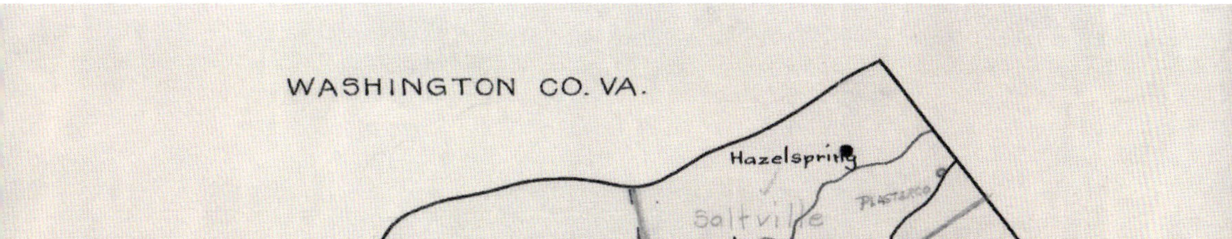

CROSSROADS OF THE COUNTY. The lines of this 1913 map depict railroad paths and use names that have since faded from modern use, like Vestal, along what is now the Virginia Creeper Trail. The thin line that runs diagonally from Hazelspring to Mendota shows the North Fork of the Holston River, long known as a shipping lane. (Courtesy of the Virginia Tech Library.)

ABINGDON'S ARTS DEPOT. Constructed in 1869 and 1870, the Abingdon Freight Station, or freight house, once served as the home of the Light Milling Company, which advertises its Purina products with a checkerboard banner in 1980. In 1990, the restored building became the Arts Depot, with working space for artists and rotating gallery displays. The Arts Depot marks the western end of Abingdon's mile-long Virginia Creeper Trail Extension. (Courtesy of David Patton.)

Glade Spring Depot. Constructed by 1857, the long-standing Glade Spring Depot survived a century that included raids during the Civil War and an 1899 railroad crash that slammed into the telegraph office. The station was built with handmade brick and used for both passengers and freight. It was torn down in the mid-1960s and replaced with a much less impressive cinder block station nearly on the same site. (Courtesy of the Virginia Tech Library.)

BANK OF GLADE SPRING. The Bank of Glade Spring building (at left) dates to 1905. The 1895 date on the brick building notes when the bank was organized at an earlier location. The building, at right, built in 1918, once housed the Farmers Exchange. By 2011, a revitalization group called Project Glade had earned grants to renovate the bank structure as part of an effort to restore the glory of Glade Spring's commercial district. (Courtesy of George Stone.)

MEADOWVIEW. Across the railroad tracks from the Meadowview Depot, the brick Meadowview Post Office building began as the County Bank, constructed in 1930, but closed in 1933, during the Depression. It later reopened as the Bank of Damascus and became a post office in 1973. The building sits on the former site of the A.B. Galliher General Store, constructed in 1909 and known for selling everything from plows to shoes. The store burned in 1926. (Courtesy of HSWCV.)

Railroad Crossing at Meadowview. In this c. 1906 image from the railroad crossing near the town square, the Meadowview Railroad Depot, built in 1883, stands out of view at right but appears to shadow the Bristol Military Band. The Meadowview United Methodist Church, built in 1898 and located in the background at left, was significantly expanded in 1955. The store building at right was constructed by Robert A. Preston in 1888, but torn down at some point after 1968 to create a parking lot. (Courtesy of HSWCV.)

Big M in Meadowview. The Big M Farm Services building (at left) took center stage around 1916 during a Laurel Steel Ranges cooking exhibit at Virginia Route 80's railroad intersection. Then operated by Ritchie-Vance and Co., the three-story store has been standing in Meadowview since 1910. The smaller Baldwin Store building at right was torn down before 1920 and replaced by the Meadowview Creamery, now used by Big M for storage. (Courtesy of HSWCV.)

ROAD THROUGH DAMASCUS. The Damascus Post Office is at far left in this 1940s postcard of Laurel Avenue. The Mock & Wright Hardware Company, at center left, was a John Deere and DuPont Paints dealer in a building later occupied by the It's a God Thing, Too Thrift Store and Mt. Rogers Outfitters. The contemporary scene captures the town's annual flea market, which kicks off Appalachian Trail Days each May. (Courtesy of the Louise Fortune Hall Collection of the Washington County Public Library.)

Downtown Damascus. Brown Brothers Sodas (at right) was a 1940s landmark on Laurel Avenue in Damascus, serving Southern Maid Ice Cream and offering curb service. The building has since been demolished, but the change allows for the contemporary view of a colorful mural, depicting the Mount Rogers National Recreation Area, on the side of the Mt. Rogers Outfitters building. (Courtesy of the Louise Fortune Hall Collection of the Washington County Public Library.)

MENDOTA. The first school in Mendota—a three-story structure owned by Masonic Lodge No. 174—was built in 1874. Called Hamilton Institute, the building was torn down in 1916, but some of its bricks were used to construct the nearby Mendota Bank building, which also housed a meeting space for the Masons. The modern Hamilton Elementary building, constructed in 1951 on the same spot as the earlier school, was closed in 1991 and later converted into a community center. (Courtesy of HSWCV.)

DUNCANSVILLE. This one-room schoolhouse served students in remote Duncansville from 1889 to 1954. Listed on most maps as Duncanville, the community name comes from a farmer named Henry Duncan who moved to an area between Brumley Gap and Hayter's Gap in 1853. The renovated schoolhouse was moved in 2000 to a new site on Stanley Road, near E.B. Stanley Middle School in Abingdon; it is now open for tours. (Courtesy of May Joe Craig.)

Hayter's Gap. What was once a dirt road for horse travel at the center of Hayter's Gap, pictured here around 1900, evolved into Virginia Route 80 leading north from Lindell to Clinch Mountain and Russell County. A community chapel, built in the 1890s (left), remains in fine condition, but a nearby farmhouse (right) has been plagued by neglect and overgrowth. This community takes its name from early settler Abraham Hayter, who arrived in the area in the 1770s. (Courtesy of HSWCV.)

Tumbling Creek. Naturally, Tumbling Creek takes its name from a rocky stream that tumbles through the nearby Clinch Mountain Wildlife Management Area. In the recent image, Little Mountain rises on the eastern horizon behind a general store once operated by Ellie Henderson. The c. 1938 image shows the store during the large June Meeting Day gathering at the nearby Tumbling Creek Primitive Church. The business, along Poor Valley Road, had closed by 2011. (Courtesy of HSWCV.)

KONNAROCK. The Konnarock Store—home of the Konnarock Post Office and once called the Mountain Store—was prosperous in the 1920s, when Konnarock was the company town of the Hassinger Lumber Company. The large-scale operation cut virgin timber from surrounding mountains and helped Konnarock boast as many as 2,000 residents. The postcard view of the town square fountain was photographed sometime after the 1950 construction of St. Matthew's Evangelical Lutheran Church (at right). (Courtesy of Bruce Waters.)

Rocktown. In the 1919 image, Charmie Rock, daughter of Samuel J. "Sam" Rock (1871–1962), stands at a fence fronting the old Rocktown store in the agricultural region of western Washington County. Samuel operated the general store at Rocktown for more than 50 years. By 2011, the business had long been closed, but the 1890s structure remained standing at Rocktown, located between the Rich Valley communities of Withers and Fleenors. (Courtesy of Donald F. White.)

Lindell. Supporting its own post office from 1883 to 1921, and located about four miles north of Meadowview, the community of Lindell may derive its name from its location in a narrow (lin) valley (dell). In 1972, the old general store at Lindell advertises Rainbo Bread and Pepsi and Coca-Cola products on its inviting front porch. This store no longer stands in the tiny community at the crossroads of Route 80 and Rich Valley Road. (Courtesy of HSWCV.)

Plasterco. In the modern image, Little Mountain rises behind the abandoned site of the company town of Plasterco, once known as Buena Vista and now returned to wilderness behind large fences. Operated by US Gypsum, the sprawling gypsum plant—shown on April 19, 1946—employed hundreds but polluted the region and was plagued by a series of cave-ins during the 1980s. The plant closed in 2000, ending about 200 years of industry on the property. (Courtesy of the Virginia Tech Library.)

Goose Pimple Junction. Russ Taylor helped erect the first Welcome to Goose Pimple Junction sign in 1955. Decades later, in 1994, the 77-year-old Taylor poses next to the Welcome to Goose Pimple Junction sign that has since faded and rusted in the community near the Bristol, Tennessee, border. The funny town name remains alive at the Goose Pimple Junction Adventure Camp for children, located near Beulah Land Baptist Church. (Photograph by Joe Tennis.)

Clinchburg. Named for neighboring Clinch Mountain, Clinchburg prospered as the company town of the Holston River Lumber Company; this crew is posing at railroad tracks and a mill around 1920. Little remains of Clinchburg's massive lumberyards, which closed after the lumber company sawed out in 1932. Today, the unincorporated town is known for its community center, established in 1986 and facing a 1918 brick store building along Old Saltworks Road. (Courtesy of Duncan's Store Collection.)

Haskell Station. A 1970s postcard depicts the excursion train of the Southwest Virginia Scenic Railroad chugging uphill from Haskell Station over the old Southern Railroad line. Haskell Station and the railroad, constructed in the late 1800s across western Washington County, have since returned to grass and trees, though the city of Bristol, Virginia, made an effort to turn the tracks into a pedestrian path called the Mendota Trail. (Courtesy of Shelby Edwards.)

BENHAMS. A freight train rolls through Benhams in 1969 along the Southern Railroad line that once linked Bristol and Benhams to Mendota and Maces Spring. A passenger train excursion ran through this area in the 1970s and 1980s. In 2004, a campaign to make the railroad at Benhams part of the Mendota Trail failed largely because of landowner resistance. Subsequently, the old line at Benhams simply became a place to park a semitruck. (Photograph by Bob McCracken.)

Wyndale. In 1960, a passenger shed stands next to the old Wyndale Train Station. Now, with the depot gone, a green sign marks Wyndale's location along the still-active railroad. The community was once called Montgomery, or Montgomery's Switch, taking its name from S.W. Montgomery, who donated land for the railroad depot. Wyndale's current name likely comes from being a "windy valley," or "wind dale," on the main line between Wallace and Abingdon. (Photograph by Bob McCracken.)

Wallace. Lying north of Bristol, Wallace became a rail stop after 1856. This c. 1900 view shows a field at far left that has since become the location of Wallace Middle School, a structure with sections dating to the 1920s. At right, a mill stands next to a long-gone pond near the railroad tracks. The steeple of Wallace United Methodist Church, founded in 1884, rises near the center in both views. (Courtesy of Karen Fitzpatrick Hall.)

Green Spring. A hillside view shows Green Spring Presbyterian Church sitting on a knob in central Washington County. This brick structure, built in the 1920s, is shown in about 1964, prior to several renovations and additions, including new rooms, a handicap-accessible ramp, and an elevator. A previous church on this site burned in 1921. The church, with its original log chapel constructed in the late 1700s, took its name from green stones found at a nearby spring. (Courtesy of HSWCV.)

Ebbing Spring. An early-1900s postcard depicts the Ebbing Spring Church, located near Lodi and the Middle Fork of the Holston River in eastern Washington County. The church takes its name from the natural wonder of the Ebbing Spring, known to ebb and flow—gushing, retreating, and then gushing again. The picket fence fronting the church has since been removed, and the church has been expanded. (Courtesy of George Stone.)

Saltville. The Old Saltville section of Washington County crosses the border into Smyth County. This 1891 view shows the King-Stuart House (center), a building dating to 1795 and once the home of William King, who dug a salt well (or salt mine) and helped the region's saltworks prosper. The L-shaped lane called Elmwood Drive now runs through Washington County's Saltville community, a town framed by mountains on the northwestern horizon. (Courtesy of the Museum of the Middle Appalachians.)

CHAPTER 2

THREE FORKS OF THE HOLSTON

NORTH FORK. At left, a grassy island rises at the center of the North Fork of the Holston River on the Smyth-Washington County border at Saltville. This c. 1891 photograph was made before the 1892 opening of the Mathieson Alkali Works, which employed thousands until the chemical operation closed in 1972. (Courtesy of the Museum of the Middle Appalachians.)

MIDDLE FORK. Little has changed over a century's time at the rapids of the Middle Fork of the Holston River at Shallowford, depicted in a 1907 color postcard, between Watauga and Osceola along US Highway 58. About five miles downstream from Shallowford, the Middle Fork meets the river's South Fork at the site of Carrickfergus, located west of present-day Alvarado and named for a town in Ireland; Hugh Neely proposed Carrickfergus as a shipping port in 1801. (Courtesy of HSWCV.)

South Fork. The support piers of Avens Bridge rise above the South Fork of the Holston River as construction continues on South Holston Lake in the late 1940s. Named for the local Avens family and completed in 1949, the 969-foot-long bridge spans the boat-friendly waters of the 24-mile-long reservoir, stretching into Sullivan County, Tennessee. Many homes have since been built on the lake's hillsides, especially on its western banks near Green Spring. (Courtesy of Donna Price.)

South Holston Lake. Using heavy equipment to construct new roads and move rock, the Tennessee Valley Authority built South Holston Lake in the late 1940s for flood control and power generation. The job, completed in 1950, produced a 1,600-foot-long dam in Sullivan County, Tennessee. It also flooded 1,600 acres in Washington County, from Alvarado to the Tennessee border, including this cove of the Grable Branch of Cox Mill Creek in isolated Denton Valley. (Courtesy of Donna Price.)

FLOOD AT TAYLORS VALLEY. The early spring floods of 1977 wreaked havoc across southwest Virginia at Grundy, Clinchport, and Chilhowie. Taylors Valley, in southeastern Washington County, was also affected, as seen in this dramatic photograph taken by Morgan Parker on Whitetop Laurel Creek at the William Lane Dunn Bridge. Normally, the bridge and the rocky creek provide a serene scene on the border of the Virginia Creeper Trail. (Courtesy of Sidney Hal Parker.)

Toole Creek Falls. Nearly all creeks draining to the North Fork of the Holston River crash across cascades in Washington County, and Toole Creek is no exception. This 10-foot-high waterfall, depicted in a 1930s postcard, is located about a mile north of a place once called Lowland and is part of a series of Toole's tumbles; it can be easily seen along Toole Creek Road when trees are missing leaves in the winter. (Courtesy of HSWCV.)

ABRAMS FALLS. Once known as the Great Falls, the 100-foot-high Abrams Falls lies on remote property near Benhams. The cataract took its name from an early homesteader sometime before 1889, the year an Abrams Falls Post Office was established. This 1930s postcard was issued when the falls were promoted as a tourist attraction, dubbed Chief Benje, or Chief Benge, Falls for a legendary Native American of the 18th century. (Postcard courtesy of V.N. "Bud" Phillips; Now photograph by Richard Kretz.)

Boating Lake. A small pond along Lakeside Drive appears to be all that remains of the Boating Lake—or McBroom's Millpond—that once covered part of northwestern Abingdon along Wolf Creek and US Highway 19/58A. The owner of this c. 1906 postcard noted that this was "nearly a mile pond . . . where we skate and canoe." The milldam broke prior to 1970 but was patched, legend says, by some boys who stole wood from a neighbor. (Courtesy of Frank Kilgore.)

Beartree Lake. Originally called the Bear Tree Complex, the 11-acre Beartree Lake was constructed near Bear Tree Gap in 1980 inside the Mount Rogers National Recreation Area. A fishing pier (at right) and sandy swimming beach (center) line the lakeshore in southeastern Washington County. The Straight Branch runs into this lake, dammed by an earth-filled wall that cost $550,000. Located about eight miles east of Damascus along US Highway 58, Beartree Recreation Area also features a campground. (Courtesy of Bill McKee.)

Edmondson Dam. The Edmondson brothers had a dam constructed on the Middle Fork of the Holston River in about 1921, forming an impoundment that became the playground for both boys and girls at Camp Pocahontas in the 1920s. The Edmondson Dam, in turn, operated as a hydroelectric facility, supplying electricity to Abingdon until 1963. Because of structural problems, the dam was partially demolished in 1982, but the site remains a frothy, 47-foot-high drop on the river. (Courtesy of HSWCV.)

CHAPTER 3

Mills of the Mountain Empire

Love-Wilkinson Mill. Time stands still at the Love-Wilkinson Mill along the South Fork of the Holston River. The "Wilkinson" comes from the family that ran the mill in the 1900s. The "Love" comes from the family of Leonidas Love, who lost his life while trying to stop a man from stealing tobacco from the store in the late 1800s. (Photograph by Bill McKee.)

OLD MILL IN DAMASCUS. The Old Mill of Damascus, located on Imboden Street, dates to about 1912 but was mostly abandoned after its heyday ended around the 1970s. The structure sat rotting for decades before it was transformed into the Damascus Old Mill Inn by investors Dennis Hutchins and Tom Potts in 2001. The mill has since survived a series of successive owners. (Courtesy of HSWCV.)

MILLPOND OF DAMASCUS. A c. 1921 postcard view of the Damascus Old Mill shows its life as Laurel Milling Company, rising three stories above Laurel Creek. A swinging bridge, shown at far right, stood below the dam until 1977. Seen from the shoreline just below the vintage vantage point, the modern-day building's restaurant, lounge, and hotel reflect in the small millpond of Laurel Creek—still a popular place to fish or wade near the center of town. (Courtesy of HSWCV.)

DAMASCUS DAM. The 10-foot-high dam at the Damascus Old Mill has changed little since it was constructed around 1912. However, the large-scale flour mill no longer resembles its former self—it has been transformed into a large eatery and 12-room lodge along Laurel Creek. Downstream of the dam, trees have shrouded the ridge overlooking the dam and millpond along Virginia Route 91 since the vintage photograph was taken in 1921. (Courtesy of HSWCV.)

Greendale Mill. The Greendale Mill, a two-story structure along Greendale Creek known for its hand-joined wooden gear train, was demolished sometime before 1970. The mill, once a center of the Greendale community in central Washington County, stood next to a large and now-dilapidated brick store building. In a 2011 image, woods and weeds have overtaken the mill's former site. (Courtesy of HSWCV.)

Holston Mill. The Holston Mill, pictured in 1974, stands near Virginia Route 802 and US Highway 19/58A above Little Moccasin Creek in north-central Washington County near the center of a community called Holston. In 2011, the two-story building that once housed gristmill and flour mill operations remains standing, but the long shed used for a sawmill—at left in the vintage view—is gone. (Courtesy of HSWCV.)

Parks Mill. David Parks purchased property in central Washington County in 1810 and built a gristmill known as Parks Mill. This three-story framed mill, photographed in 1974, dates to about 1870. The property has since evolved into a rustic restaurant and tourist attraction, serving ice cream and barbecue in a natural picnic setting along the rippling waters of Fifteenmile Creek between Abingdon and South Holston Lake. (Courtesy of HSWCV.)

White's Mill. Icicles drip from the waterwheel at White's Mill, an icon of Washington County, located about four miles north of downtown Abingdon. Portions of the mill may date to the late 1790s, though some historians affix a time period for the current mill to about 1840. The name comes from Col. James White, who acquired the property in 1838 along Toole Creek. The mill's wooden millrace was removed as part of a long-term restoration project in 2007. (Photograph by Bill McKee.)

CHAPTER 4

BACK ROADS AND BYWAYS

WHITETOP MOUNTAIN. Winding from Grayson County into the southeastern corner of Washington County and dead-ending in Smyth County, Virginia's highest navigable road reaches a mile-high elevation on Whitetop Mountain. The only way to reach this gravel lane, Forest Service Road 89, in Washington County is to travel through Grayson County. The Appalachian Trail crosses the peak of Whitetop, which reaches a 5,520-foot elevation. (Courtesy of HSWCV.)

ROAD TO KONNAROCK. A c. 1920 postcard depicts the "Road to Konnarock" as near Abingdon, though the logging commuwnity of Konnarock actually lies about 20 miles from the courthouse town. The thoroughfare at far left is now called Konnarock Road, which meanders along Whitetop Laurel Creek about a half-mile east of US Highway 58. The earlier rock wall is gone, but a similar structure stands in its place on this popular trout stream. (Courtesy of HSWCV.)

Laurel Avenue. This view of Laurel Avenue in Damascus, pictured in both 1921 and 2011, shows the Damascus Motor Company's garage at far right, now home to Blue Blaze Bike Rental & Shuttle. The homes at left, outlined by white picket fences, have since become a lot for a car dealership. Laurel Avenue doubles as part of US Highway 58, the longest road in Virginia, which stretches 500 miles between Virginia Beach and Cumberland Gap. (Courtesy of HSWCV.)

ROUTE 58 AT SHALLOWFORD. The small Shallowford Bridge crossed the Middle Fork of the Holston River when this folksy postcard circulated in the early 1900s. The cabin and the wild trees in the foreground are gone, having been replaced by an ongoing construction project, shown here in 2011, to build four lanes on US Highway 58 between Abingdon and Damascus. The center structure in the modern photograph is a sprawling water-treatment plant built by the Goodson-Kinderhook Water Authority in 1975 and 1976. (Courtesy of Shelby Edwards.)

View of Whitetop. The white field of grass that inspired the name of Whitetop Mountain—sometimes spelled "White Top"—can be seen near the Honey Locust Knobs (left) at a crest of US Highway 58 between Watauga and Shallowford. The field in the foreground has been altered from the 1930s postcard scene by a road-widening project to build four lanes on US 58, which encroached on lawns and erased roadside homes. (Courtesy of Joe Tennis.)

Route 11 at Cedarville. This 1961 postcard shows C.H. Ruth's photograph of the Last Wagon West along US Highway 11 near Cedarville. The Last Wagon West was a cross-country trip planned and executed by Leon Gillis, who built a wagon and then, along with his family, drove it 3,000 miles across the United States, from Virginia to California. Road signs in the scene show State Route 80 leading to Meadowview and US Highway 11 pointing the way to Roanoke and Chilhowie. This postcard predates the 1960s construction of Interstate 81 through the heart of Washington County. (Courtesy of Shelby Edwards.)

Bristol to Washington Highway. In Abingdon, Colonial Road passes by the Hurt House, now named Retirement, at the site of the footbridge and ford on Wolf Creek—which was called Hurt's Creek when this postcard was issued in 1907. The ford no longer exists; a new pedestrian bridge is now in place slightly to the right of this scene. The north-south route of US Highway 11 parallels Colonial Road. (Courtesy of HSWCV.)

Courthouse Town Pit Stop. A snowstorm blankets the Esso Gas Station in this mid-20th century photograph taken from the Abingdon crossroads of Main Street and Tanner Road. A pole at the service station shows the mileage to Hansonville (13), Norton (59), Tazewell (65), and Roanoke (146). An upscale restaurant called Rain stands at this site in 2011. At left in both scenes is the James Longley/James K. Gibson House, originally two homes dating to the 1790s that are now joined. (Courtesy of David Patton.)

ACTORS CROSSING. The Slow Actors Crossing signs, a novelty on Abingdon's Main Street in the 1950s, were later replaced by crosswalks near the Barter Theatre. Barter's founder, Robert Porterfield (not shown), posed in alternate shots of the vintage scene; this 1959 image shows actors Patricia Gilbert Read and Dennis J. King. Behind them, *Gigi* is advertised as a "charming comedy" on the theater's marquee; the contemporary marquee advertises *Beauty and the Beast*. (Courtesy of the Barter Theatre.)

Gate City Highway. In this c. 1940 scene looking east on US Highway 58, or Gate City Highway, near Three Springs, Olean Cowden poses on the front porch of the home of Agnes and Woodrow Dishner. The road width has hardly changed, but the porch has been rebuilt and the hillside trees have grown considerably along this east-west route. The billboard in the vintage photograph advertises the Hotel Virginia in nearby Bristol. (Courtesy of Jerry Ivey.)

CHAPTER 5

OVERNIGHT ACCOMMODATIONS

MOUNTAIN VIEW CABINS. In this c. 1940 image, the Mountain View Cabins stand near the southwest base of Walker Mountain at US Highway 58. A Sinclair Gasoline station occupies the center building; the structure at right houses a Bar-B-Cue Sandwich restaurant. The cabins, later called Mountain View Court, had closed by 2011. (Courtesy of Jerry Ivey and V.N. "Bud" Phillips.)

Camp Wildwood. In the early 1900s, motels and lodges popped up along the length of Lee Highway/US 11, including the more than 30 miles stretching through Washington County. Among these was Camp Wildwood, advertised on the back of this 1947 postcard as having "running water, showers, meals, camping tables, trailer space, service, cleanliness . . . [and] courtesy." The main lodge, still standing on the road between Abingdon and Meadowview, has since become a private residence fronted by a carport. (Courtesy of Shelby Edwards.)

Broadway Oaks. Several of the lodge units still stand at the 1940s location of the Broadway Oaks Motor Court & Grill, now an apartment complex along Lee Highway/US 11 near Abingdon. A convenience store called Mike's Pit Stop once operated at the modern site of the old grill, which specialized in steaks and chicken. The original grass island fronting the restaurant remains, but is overgrown with weeds along the four-lane US 11, near Interstate 81's Exit 13. (Courtesy of David Patton.)

Robert E. Lee Motel. Opened in 1946 near Bristol, the Robert E. Lee Motel housed a restaurant once operated by Col. Harland Sanders, founder of Kentucky Fried Chicken. Years later, the motel graced the cover of musician Clint Miller's 2006 concept album, *Ballad of a Modern Day Cowboy*. The crumbling motel was demolished in 2009, but within a year, its iconic sign was restored and resurrected at R.C.'s Storage, located on the opposite side of Lee Highway. (Courtesy of Shelby Edwards.)

Hotels on Wall Street. In the early days of passenger trains, the Depot Square section of Abingdon's Wall Street, shown here around 1914, retained a New Orleans–style look with the presence of the Hattie House Hotel, right, an 1885 structure that was renovated—about a century after it was built—as the Abingdon Mercantile. At left are the towering Belmont Hotel and adjacent shops; all were torn down after 1981 to construct the Abingdon Post Office. (Courtesy of HSWCV.)

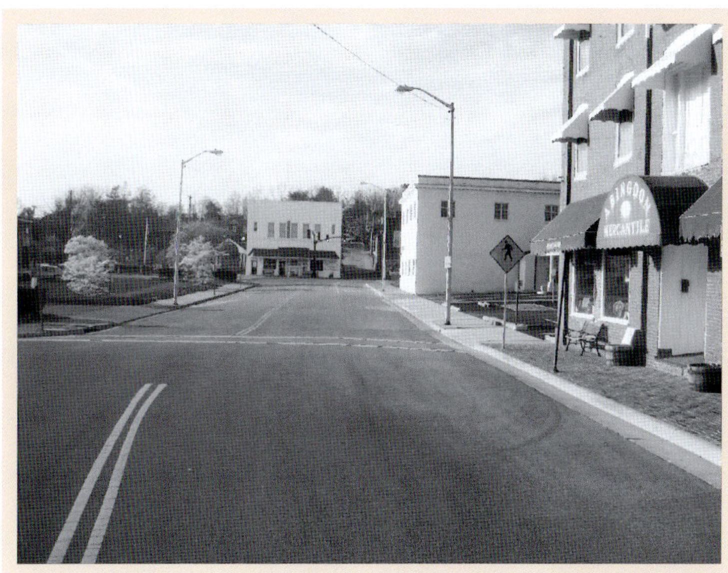

The Martha. Constructed in 1832, the Martha Washington Inn was once the family home of Francis Preston. It became a women's college by the onset of the Civil War, in the 1860s, and attracted a string of ghostly legends. This image shows the building as it transitioned from home to college, long before a series of renovations and additions turned it into a luxury hotel famous for its antique furnishings and magnificent amenities. (Courtesy of HSWCV.)

CHAPTER 6

LEGENDS AND LANDMARKS

THE GREAT CHANNELS. A series of unique rock outcrops called the Great Channels became part of the Channels State Forest in Washington County in 2008, not long after The Nature Conservancy acquired the property along the crest of Clinch Mountain. These odd structures resemble a maze or roofless cave. (Photograph by Joe Tennis.)

Atop Clinch Mountain. In 1960, one year before their wedding, Gerald and Nancy Booher pose below the Mendota Fire Tower, near Fugate Gap, at an elevation of about 3,000 feet on Clinch Mountain. These hard-to-reach outcrops still attract sightseers wanting to gaze west toward the Moccasin Valley communities of Collinwood and Fugates Hill, in Russell County, and perhaps even as far west as Castlewood and St. Paul. (Courtesy of HSWCV.)

VIRGINIA'S ROOFTOP. From Abingdon to Loves Mill, the northeastern portion of Washington County affords priceless views of Virginia's Rooftop—Mount Rogers and Whitetop, popping out of the horizon along the county's borders with Grayson and Smyth Counties. Ironically, the taller of the two—Mount Rogers (left), at 5,729 feet—appears shorter than the 5,520-foot-high Whitetop Mountain. One of the best views is from the cemetery above Emory & Henry College. (Courtesy of HSWCV.)

Emory & Henry College. Founded in 1836, Emory & Henry College ranks as the oldest institution of higher education in southwest Virginia. Throughout its history, buildings have come and gone, including the William Morrow Science Building, constructed by the 1889–1890 academic year. The building was razed in 1956 and remains an empty area on campus, fronting the college's Kelly Library. (Courtesy of HSWCV.)

Virginia Highlands Community College. Virginia Highlands Community College, located just off Interstate 81, first held classes on its present campus during the 1970–1971 academic year. At the time, the college's administration building stood amid blank fields and freshly-planted trees. Today, those trees obscure the landscape, and a half-dozen more buildings stand on campus, including the 1998 addition—the Southwest Virginia Higher Education Center, located in the center of the contemporary photograph. (Courtesy of Anne Dunham.)

Retirement. Like many historic homes, Retirement appears to grow younger as more research is revealed. Known as the Hurt House in the 1930s, when this postcard circulated, it was believed that the home had been built in 1808. More recently, historians have surmised the brick structure was constructed just a few years later. The Town of Abingdon has since acquired the property and opened it as part of an interpretive center at this site, the head of the Overmountain Victory National Historic Trail. (Courtesy of HSWCV.)

Washington County Courthouse. Topped with a towering cupola that dominates downtown Abingdon, the Washington County Courthouse was built in 1868–1869 to replace an earlier structure that burned in 1864, in the midst of the Civil War. This c. 1895 view shows dusty streets and horseback riders trotting past the building's stately columns. A 1992 courthouse expansion (at left) occupies the lot of the J.A. Barrow Cheap Cash Store building, which burned down in 1925. (Courtesy of HSWCV.)

ALTAMONT. Walter Preston built Altamont at what is now northeastern Abingdon in 1860, and it is rumored that his ghost would linger on the lawn, working in the garden on stormy nights. Eleanor Roosevelt's father, Elliott Roosevelt, often visited Altamont while living in Abingdon in the 1890s. The stately home was demolished in 1995, though its former perch, on a grassy knoll overlooking US Highway 11 near Christ the King Catholic Church and St. John Lutheran Church, has remained vacant. (Photograph by Bill McKee.)

Acklin. In spring, dogwoods bloom on the lawn of the handsome Acklin, or Ackland, built in 1859 by Abingdon merchant James C. Greenway. Confederate general John Hunt Morgan used Acklin as a headquarters in 1864. The brick home's name comes from the Acklin family, who owned the land in the early 1800s. Owners have included Wilton Egerton Mingea, developer of the Virginia-Carolina Railway, the former tracks of which are now the path of the Virginia Creeper Trail. (Courtesy of HSWCV.)

Walnut Grove. Sitting at the edge of Bristol, in the commercially developed area off of Exit 7 on Interstate 81, the two-story Walnut Grove has been referred to by some historians as the oldest frame house in Washington County. Robert Preston, the county's first land surveyor, had the house built in the 1790s near the crest of a field draining to Beaver Creek. Walnut Grove is in the deep distance in the vintage image, which shows an agricultural gathering around 1950. (Courtesy of Bristol Historical Association.)

Brook Hall. Built by 1826 for Col. William Byars, the brick landmark called Brook Hall rises along Lee Highway, slightly south of Glade Spring. The massive mansion—visited by Andrew Jackson and several governors—fell into disrepair by the early 1900s. Brook Hall was restored by later owners and was listed in the Virginia Landmarks Register in 1997. The house features several chimneys, a couple dozen rooms, and custom-built mantels. (Courtesy of HSWCV.)

Barter Theatre. Standing on Abingdon's Main Street since the 1830s, the brick Barter Theatre building was constructed as a church and later used as a municipal building; the words "City Hall" remain in stone atop the curved front entrance. The landmark was known as Abingdon's Opera House when this postcard was mailed in 1909, just 24 years before theatergoers began bartering items like beans, tomatoes, milk, snakes, turtles, and cottage cheese in exchange for admission to shows. (Courtesy of George Stone.)

Moonlite Theatre. The Moonlite Theatre's letters got a touch-up in 1989, just as the theater turned 40 years old. Opened on June 9, 1949, along the Lee Highway between Abingdon and Bristol, the Moonlite attracts moviegoers throughout the summer months. It ranks as the last survivor among Washington County's drive-in movie theaters, including the Summit at Glade Spring and the Laurel at Damascus. The Moonlite was listed in the Virginia Landmarks Register in 2007. (Courtesy of Bill McKee.)

Tin Bridge Trestle. In the c. 1907 image, a train crew stands atop the replacement span of the Tin Bridge Trestle, a structure on the old Salt Branch Railroad between Plasterco and Clinchburg. By 2011, a new deck was installed on the Tin Bridge Trestle, and the span was incorporated into the ever-evolving path of the Salt Trail, a nine-mile-long pedestrian path linking Saltville to Glade Spring. (Courtesy of the Museum of the Middle Appalachians.)

Duff House. Photographed around 1907, the home of Thomas Duff and his wife, Ann Elizabeth Spraker Ketron Duff, was constructed near the South Fork of the Holston River. The house can be seen from the Virginia Creeper Trail, just east of the Alvarado Depot. The modern image shows a century's worth of changes, including siding and a new roof, though the majestic rural character of the home remains. (Courtesy of HSWCV.)

Tornadoes. A rare F2 tornado ripped apart Fred Buck's house in the Stonewall Heights section of Abingdon on March 4, 1944. Nearly 70 years later, a horrific EF3 tornado tore an 18-mile path across the county from near Abingdon to Glade Spring and Plum Creek. The Now image shows a damaged home on Lee Highway in Glade Spring only hours after the twister touched down around 1:00 a.m. on April 28, 2011, killing three people. (Courtesy of HSWCV.)

CHAPTER 7

The Creeper

Twister Trashes Trestle. As April 27 faded into April 28 in 2011, the 650-foot-long Trestle No. 7 crumbled when a series of tornadoes spun into Washington County. This trestle spanned a ravine near the River Knobs east of Watauga. It was built in the late 1800s and used for train traffic on the Virginia-Carolina Railway, nicknamed The Virginia Creeper—the remnants of the line are now the 34-mile-long Virginia Creeper Trail. (Courtesy of Richard Smith.)

South Holston Trestle. Photographer Ken Marsh captured a steam train carrying manganese on the Abingdon Branch of the Norfolk & Western Railway in this June 30, 1956, photograph of the South Holston Trestle. The 529-foot-long span marks the northernmost gateway to South Holston Lake, a reservoir with levels that fluctuate seasonally. Guardrails have since been placed on the sides of the bridge to accommodate walkers, bicyclists, equestrians, and cross-country skiers on the Virginia Creeper Trail. (Courtesy of Ken Marsh.)

Alvarado Depot. Bob McCracken recorded the original Alvarado Depot on color slide film in 1960. The green-and-white station, which once housed a US post office, stood at the approximate site of the Alvarado Depot replica, constructed in 2011 to offer restrooms and a meeting facility on the Virginia Creeper Trail. The vintage view looks northwest, with the railroad at the right. The contemporary view looks in the opposite direction, toward Holston Mountain, showing a church and store at right. (Courtesy of Bob McCracken.)

Damascus Depot. The Damascus Town Park provides a major stop at the halfway point of the Virginia Creeper Trail, boasting a playground, a gazebo, and a railroad caboose. The site of the old Damascus Depot, seen here in 1964, remains a blank patch of grass at the park. What was once a spur running along the depot, however, has since become an in-town section of the Appalachian Trail, a 2,181-mile-long path that stretches from Georgia to Maine. (Courtesy of Ken Marsh.)

Laureldale. The Virginia-Carolina Railway's Laureldale depot (far left), located near the confluence of Tennessee Laurel and Whitetop Laurel Creeks, prospered with lumber harvests in the early 1900s. Here, the path of the V-C Railway runs to the bottom left while the Laurel Railway spur curves right, running south to Tennessee. This site has since returned to woods along the Virginia Creeper Trail east of Virginia Route 91. (Courtesy of the Louise Fortune Hall Collection of the Washington County Public Library.)

Whitetop Laurel Falls. The president of the Virginia-Carolina Railway, Wilton Egerton Mingea, arranged an excursion for Abingdon-area officials on the Virginia-Carolina Railway around 1905, with a stop at Whitetop Laurel Falls, between Damascus and Taylors Valley. The trout-stocked creek drops about 10 feet at this waterfall, a popular place for fly fishermen and overheated trail-users; it is located along the trail about one mile west of the Straight Branch parking lot, just off US Highway 58. (Courtesy of Jerry Goodpasture and HSWCV.)

Taylors Valley. At an elevation of 2,390 feet, tracks across the highlands of Taylors Valley impose a certain dominance on the land in this 1951 photograph that catches the heavy traffic during opening day of trout season on Whitetop Laurel Creek. The two-story Taylors Valley depot has since been torn down; a railroad camp car was later put on the same place. The rugged railroad has been transformed into the bicycle-friendly Virginia Creeper Trail. (Courtesy of Sidney Hal Parker.)

GREEN COVE. Built in 1914, the Green Cove Depot served southeastern Washington County as a train station, post office, and store, but it appears abandoned—and in need of its classic green-and-white paint job—in this 1964 photograph. Adele Buchanan Edwards, a daughter of station agent William M. Buchanan, donated the station to the US Forest Service in 1991, and it was later renovated for use as a visitors center located near US Highway 58 on the Virginia Creeper Trail. (Courtesy of Ken Marsh.)

About the Author

A Radford University graduate and a resident of Washington County, Virginia, Joe Tennis has contributed thousands of articles and photographs to *Blue Ridge Country, Bristol Herald Courier, The Roanoke Times, The Virginian-Pilot, Kingsport Times-News*, *Virginia Living*, and *Appalachian Voice*. He has also written for *Virginia Wine Lover*.

The author's articles on the people and places of Washington County have also appeared in newspapers across Virginia, including the *Richmond Times-Dispatch*, and have won numerous awards from the Virginia Press Association and Tennessee Press Association.

All of the author's previous books feature Washington County, including *Southwest Virginia Crossroads: An Almanac of Place Names and Places to See* (Overmountain Press); *The Marble and Other Ghost Tales of Tennessee and Virginia* (Backyard Books); *Beach to Bluegrass: Places to Brake on Virginia's Longest Road* (Overmountain Press); Images of America: *Sullivan County, Tennessee* (Arcadia Publishing); *Haunts of Virginia's Blue Ridge Highlands* (History Press); and *Finding Franklin: Mystery of the Lost State Capitol* (Backyard Books).

Since 2004, the author has spoken to thousands of adults and children, including appearances at the Library of Virginia in Richmond; the Virginia Festival of the Book in Charlottesville; the Washington County Public Library in Abingdon; civic clubs and fraternal organizations; and in elementary schools across Washington County at Meadowview, Abingdon, Greendale, Watauga, and Rhea Valley.

The author has also taught a Legends of Local History class for the College of Older Adults at the Southwest Virginia Higher Education Center in Abingdon and was named an honorary citizen of Abingdon when addressing the Historical Society of Washington County, Virginia, in 2005.